SCHOLASTIC

Data Collection Mini-Books:
Science, Math, and Social Studies

BY CONSTANCE J. LEUENBERGER

D1530201

New York • Toronto • London • Auckland • Sydney
Mexico City • New Delhi • Hong Kong • Buenos Aires

Teaching
Resources

This book is for Rhonda, very sweet niece of mine.

"What's in the Lost and Found?" by Joan Novelli. Copyright © 2006
by Joan Novelli. Used by permission of the author.
Edited by Joan Novelli.
Cover design by Jason Robinson.
Interior design by Holly Grundon.
Interior art by Maxie Chambliss, Cary Pillo, Anne Kennedy, and James Graham Hale.

ISBN-13: 978-0-439-58063-2
ISBN-10: 0-439-58063-3

Contents

Math Mini-Books

Science Mini-Books

Social Studies Mini-Books

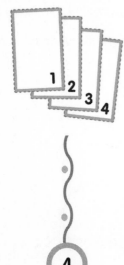

Introduction

Children are full of wonder for the world around them, from the puddles they splash in to the rocks and other treasures that sometimes fill their pockets. The world is one big classroom for these young learners, as they collect, organize, display, and study data they gather on a daily basis. The data collection lessons and mini-books in the pages that follow encourage children's natural love of exploring and learning, and their desire to create. Approaching learning as a process, these mini-books foster interactive learning and engage all learners, challenging every student to make new discoveries and build skills and learn concepts in math, literacy, science, and more. (For information on how the content of the mini-books connects with the standards, see page 5.)

Each of the 15 mini-books encourages children to use active learning and hands-on experiences as they construct knowledge about the world. A lesson for each mini-book provides step-by-step support for guiding children in conducting their research and analyzing data, to create books that they can revisit again and again. Children not only learn about specific concepts, such as standard and nonstandard measurement and properties of water, but also hone reading and writing skills. You will find the mini-books help to scaffold children's learning in the area of conducting research and recording their observations. As children pose questions and gather data about themselves and their surroundings, they begin to make sense of their world, forming connections between math, science, and social studies concepts and deepening understandings.

How to Make and Use the Mini-Books

The mini-books are fun and easy to make, and gratifying for emergent readers to use. Simply photocopy a class set of all pages of the mini-book. Cut along the dashed lines to separate the mini-book pages. Put each set of pages in order and staple to bind. The mini-books are now ready to use.

The mini-books are designed for use over the course of one or two lessons, depending upon students' age and ability level, and can be used in any order to help you meet the needs of your science, math, and social studies curriculum. You may want to customize some of the mini-books by adding details—for example, "Our Favorite Authors" (page 76) includes space for you to add another author to a class survey. Other ideas for customizing the mini-books include adding extra pages for students to gather more data, or changing the activities slightly to better accommodate your students.

Preview the books with students before beginning the data collection activities. As you read the mini-book aloud, discuss new vocabulary and concepts. In the lesson pages, you'll find more ideas for teaching with the mini-books, including:

- step-by-step plans for using the mini-books with children.

- ideas for extending students' learning.

- book links to enrich learning experiences.

Incorporating Graphic Organizers

Many of the data collection mini-books incorporate the use of graphic organizers, such as charts, tables, and graphs. For example, in "Measure the School" (page 25), children complete a chart, then use the information in it to make comparisons about the number of steps it takes to get from the classroom to various places in the school. In "How Are Trees Alike? How Are Trees Different?" (page 33), children observe trees and use charts to organize and compare information about identifying characteristics. And in "Our Favorite Authors" (page 76), children graph results of a survey, then use the graph as a tool to assess their data.

Research supports the use of graphic organizers as effective instructional tools. Using graphic organizers has been shown to improve student learning, including in reading comprehension, development and organization of ideas, and retention and recall of information. (Institute for the Advancement of Research in Education, 2003)

Connections to the Standards: Math

The National Council of Teachers of Mathematics (NCTM) has outlined learning expectations for grades preK–12 in *Principles and Standards for School Mathematics* (NCTM, 2000). *The Curriculum Focal Points for Prekindergarten Through Grade 8 Mathematics: A Quest for Coherence* (NCTM, 2006) identifies, among these learning expectations, key concepts and skills for emphasis at each grade level. These curriculum focal points are designed to help teachers organize curriculum so that skills are developed in a structured, meaningful way. Each focal point, important for further study of mathematics both inside and outside of school, emphasizes the best practices to help children learn mathematics and connects with what is taught in earlier and later grade levels.

You will find the mini-books in this collection provide support for the standards and curriculum focal points for grades K–1 (see chart, below) and make important connections to other areas of mathematics, including the process standards (problem solving, reasoning and proof, communication, connections, and representations).

Mini-Book Title	Number/ Operations	Algebra	Geometry	Measurement	Data Analysis & Probability
Count the School	X				X
What's in the Lost and Found?	X	X			X
What's in a Name?	X	X			X
Measure the School	X		X	X	X
Seasons Full of Birthdays	X	X		X	X
How Are Trees Alike? How Are Trees Different?	X	X	X	X	X
Eating Lunch With the Five Food Groups	X	X			X
Discovering Rocks	X	X	X	X	X
How Many Water Drops?	X			X	X
Will It Sink? Will It Float?		X			X
School Helpers	X	X			X
Fire Safety	X	X			X
Mapping the School	X		X	X	X
Our Favorite Times	X	X		X	X
Our Favorite Authors	X	X			X

After students have completed their data collection with a mini-book, use repeated readings with partners, small groups, or individually to allow students to demonstrate the new information they have learned and improve their reading skills. Children can also color the mini-book illustrations. Place completed books on display in the classroom reading center or other centers, as appropriate. Invite children to explore their classmates' mini-books to make comparisons and deepen understanding.

Connections to the Standards: Language Arts

In addition to supporting the math standards, the mini-books are aligned with the following reading and writing standards outlined by Mid-continent Research for Education and Learning (McREL), an organization that collects and synthesizes national and state K–12 curriculum standards.

Reading Standards

- Uses meaning clues to aid comprehension and make predictions about content.
- Understands level-appropriate sight words and vocabulary.
- Uses reading skills and strategies to understand a variety of informational texts.
- Relates new information to prior knowledge and experience.

Writing Standards

- Uses drawings to express thoughts, feelings, and ideas.
- Writes for different purposes.
- Gathers and uses information for research purposes.
- Generates questions about topics of personal interest.
- Uses a variety of sources to gather information.

Connections to the Standards: Science

The mini-books also connect with a number of the National Science Education Content Standards, the criteria intended to guide the quality of science teaching and learning in this country. The standards describe which science concepts children at different grade levels should understand and skills they should develop.

- **Science as Inquiry:** Scientific investigations involve asking and answering a question, observing, making predictions, comparing and contrasting, classifying, using tools to measure, gathering data, and recording and communicating results.

- **Life Science:** Plants have different structures that serve different functions in growth and survival.

- **Science in Personal & Social Perspectives:** Nutrition is essential to health; students should understand how eating a variety of foods contributes to health.

- **Earth Science:** Earth materials include solid rocks that have different physical properties.

- **Physical Science:** Substances such as liquids have many observable properties including size, shape, and color, and the ability to react with other substances.

Mini-Lesson: Tallying

Several of the mini-books, for example, "Count the School" (page 8), and "Seasons Full of Birthdays" (page 29), have children use tallying as a way to keep track of the data they collect. Tallying also lets children practice one-to-one correspondence in counting. Before children use any of the mini-books that involve tallying, introduce them to this useful skill.

1. Begin by modeling tallying during a morning meeting (or other opening exercise). Tally how many days you have been in school for the month. For each day, invite students to notice how you form the tally mark— either by making a vertical line or a diagonal line. Reinforce that the first four lines in a bundle of five are evenly spaced vertical lines, with every fifth line drawn diagonally across the first four (see right). If you tally ten or more days, draw a circle around every two sets of five to visually indicate 10.

2. When students begin to understand the process, invite the helper of the day to take over adding the tally mark for the day. Each day, invite children to explain why the tally is vertical or diagonal and why.

3. Later, give students the opportunity to try their own hand at tallying things in their environment. In the beginning stages, it is easiest to use tallies with concrete objects. This allows children to actually see the one-to-one correspondence between a tally mark and the thing they are tallying (such as the number of children or windows in the classroom). It's important that students understand that each tally mark matches up with the item they are tallying (so five windows should easily be seen as five tally marks, and so on).

4. Provide further practice by weaving a tallying exercise into other parts of the day. When students arrive in the morning, for example, have them use tallies to indicate their lunch choice. Invite students to circle sets of tallies to show 10.

Bibliography

Duke, N. K., and Bennett-Armistead, V. S. (2003). *Reading & writing informational text in the primary grades: Research-based practices*, New York: Scholastic.

Institute for the Advancement of Research in Education (2003). Graphic organizers: A review of scientifically based research. Charleston: WV: Appalachia Educational Laboratory.

Mid-continent Research for Education and Learning (2004). *Content knowledge: A compendium of standards and benchmarks for K–12 education.* Aurora, CO: Mid-continent Research for Education and Learning.

National Council of Teachers of Mathematics. (2006). *Curriculum focal points for prekindergarten through grade 8 mathematics*. Reston, VA: National Council of Teachers of Mathematics.

National Council of Teachers of Mathematics. (2000). *Principles and standards for school mathematics*. Reston, VA: National Council of Teachers of Mathematics.

National Research Council (1996). *National science education content standards*. Washington, D.C.: National Academy of Sciences.

Count the School

Children travel the school predicting and counting, and later organize and compare the data they've collected.

Teaching With the Mini-Book

1. It's easier with this mini-book to ask children to make all their predictions first, then count the various items around their school. Beginning on page 2, invite children to predict and record how many steps are at the front of the school.

2. Invite children to predict how many doors, clocks, mailboxes, and pets there are in the school, and ask them to record their predictions on pages 3 through 6.

3. Explain to students that the best way to keep track of counting a number of things is to make tally marks (see mini-lesson, page 7). Encourage children to make tally marks in the "How Many?" cells on the charts, totaling them when they are finished.

4. Group children in pairs (or any other way that works best), and have them walk around the school to count the items listed on pages 2 through 6 of the mini-book. When the counting is complete, students can return to the classroom to complete the mini-book.

5. Invite children to fill in the chart on page 7 to compare their predictions with the actual number of items they counted. Using the chart on page 7, encourage children to complete the mini-book (page 8) by recording what they counted the most and fewest of, as well as writing about something they learned that surprised them.

Extending Students' Learning

Count the Classroom: Generate a class book based on the mini-book. During a shared writing time, invite students to come up with things they would like to count in the classroom. Turn these ideas into a class-made mini-book called "Count the Classroom." Make a copy for each child and encourage students to complete it. Students can compare the data they collected to learn more.

Getting Started

This mini-book activity works best when children pair up. In advance, let staff members know that children will be traveling around the building counting items. Be sure to read the mini-book ahead of time and make any adjustments that may be necessary for the book to work at your school.

Book Links

More Than One by Miriam Schlein (Greenwillow, 1996). Illustrations encourage problem solving and higher-order thinking skills as children discover that a whale is one, but also that a pair of shoes can be one, as well as a week of seven days and a baseball team with nine players.

Reese's Pieces Count by Fives by Jerry Pallotta (Scholastic, 2000). Opportunities for one-to-one correspondence, counting by fives, and using yummy food for math fill this colorful book.

Count the School

Name _____

Date _____

(1)

Data Collection Mini-Books: Science, Math, and Social Studies © 2007 by Constance J. Leuenberger, Scholastic Teaching Resources

Count the school!

I predict there are _____ steps at the front of the school.

Count and tally.

Item	My Prediction	How Many?
Steps		

There are _____ more _____ fewer steps than I predicted.

(2)

Count the school!

I predict there are _____ doors in the hallway.

Count and tally.

Item	My Prediction	How Many?
Doors		

There are _____ more _____ fewer   doors than I predicted.

3

Data Collection Mini-Books: Science, Math, and Social Studies © 2007 by Constance J. Leuenberger, Scholastic Teaching Resources

Count the school!

I predict there are _____ clocks in the school.

Count and tally.

Item	My Prediction	How Many?
Digital Clocks		
Hand Clocks		

Total Clocks: _____ + _____ = _____ clocks

4

Count the school!

I predict there are _____ mailboxes in the office.

Count and tally.

Item	My Prediction	How Many?
Mailboxes		

There are _____ more _____ fewer mailboxes than I predicted.

5

Count the school!

I predict there are _____ pets   in the school.

Count and tally.

Item	My Prediction	How Many?
Fish		
Hamster		
Other		

Write a number sentence to tell how many pets.

6

Fill in the chart.

Item	My Prediction	How Many?
Steps		
Doors		
Clocks		
Mailboxes		
Pets		

Data Collection Mini-Books: Science, Math, and Social Studies © 2007 by Constance J. Leuenberger, Scholastic Teaching Resources   page 12

Data Collection Mini-Books: Science, Math, and Social Studies © 2007 by Constance J. Leuenberger, Scholastic Teaching Resources

Survey Results

1. I counted more _____ than _____ .

2. I counted fewer _____ than _____ .

3. I was surprised by _____

_____ .

What's in the Lost and Found?

Children collect, classify, and organize data they gather from the school's Lost and Found.

Teaching With the Mini-Book

1. Generate discussion about what happens to things when they are lost. Where is a good place to look for lost items at school?

2. Tell children that they will be using the school's Lost and Found to collect data. Invite them to make hypotheses about what they will find in the Lost and Found and record these ideas on pages 2 and 3 of the mini-book.

3. Review pages 4 through 9 and let children make predictions about how many of each item pictured they will find in the Lost and Found (hats, shoes, jackets, and so on). Use page 10 to make predictions about a new item. Have children fill in the chart on each page (4–10) to record their predictions.

4. Visit the Lost and Found to complete pages 4 through 10. Remind children to color a picture for each item they find, and to record the total on the chart.

5. Have children review pages 4 through 10 of the mini-book and then complete the chart on page 11 to compare data. Invite children to organize their data on page 12, numbering the items from most to fewest. Wrap up the investigation by having them complete the last two observations on page 12.

Extending Students' Learning

- **Share the Information:** Did children find a large number of jackets, or a very special item? Have them make and display "Found" posters based on their data. During the daily announcements, children can also announce items found, giving details to help children recognize items that may belong to them.

- **Sorting and Classifying:** Invite students to brainstorm ways to sort the items in the Lost and Found. Is there a way to make it easier to find missing items (for example, by hanging like items together, or placing them in labeled boxes or crates)? Extend it further, and take on organizing the Lost and Found as a community service project.

Getting Started

You can decide if it will be easier to have the class visit the Lost and Found together, in small groups, or two at a time. In advance, check the Lost and Found to make sure that the number of items there is manageable for children to count. If not, set aside a number of items for children to use in their research.

Book Links

Knuffle Bunny by Mo Willems (Hyperion, 2004). Trixie loses Knuffle Bunny at the Laundromat, then has trouble communicating this to her father.

The Lost and Found by Mark Teague (Scholastic, 1998). Two boys follow a girl on a fantasy trip into an underground world of a school's Lost and Found.

What's in the Lost and Found?

Draw a picture of things you think you'll find in the Lost and Found.

2

What's in the Lost and Found?

Name _____

Date _____

1

What's in the Lost and Found?

Fill in the chart to predict how many

hats .

Color a hat for each one you find.

Fill in the chart to tell how many hats.

Item	My Prediction	How Many?
Hats		

4

I. What do you think you'll find the most of?

_____

2. What do you think you'll find the fewest of?

_____

3. Do you think you will find anything that belongs to you? Explain.

_____

_____

_____

3

6

What's in the Lost and Found?

Fill in the chart to predict how many

jackets .

Color a jacket for each one you find.

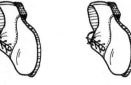

Fill in the chart to tell how many jackets.

Item	My Prediction	How Many?
Jackets		

5

What's in the Lost and Found?

Fill in the chart to predict how many

shoes  .

Color a shoe for each one you find.

Fill in the chart to tell how many shoes.

Item	My Prediction	How Many?
Shoes		

What's in the Lost and Found?

Fill in the chart to predict how many

books .

Color a book for each one you find.

Fill in the chart to tell how many books.

Item	My Prediction	How Many?
Books		

Data Collection Mini-Books: Science, Math, and Social Studies © 2007 by Joan Novelli, Scholastic Teaching Resources   page 17

Data Collection Mini-Books: Science, Math, and Social Studies © 2007 by Joan Novelli, Scholastic Teaching Resources

What's in the Lost and Found?

Fill in the chart to predict how many

lunch boxes .

Color a lunch box for each one you find.

Fill in the chart to tell how many lunch boxes.

Item	My Prediction	How Many?
Lunch Boxes 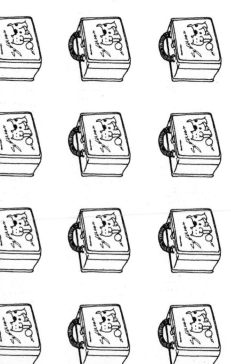		

What's in the Lost and Found?

Fill in the chart to predict how many

_____ .

Draw a picture for each one you find.

Fill in the chart to tell how many.

Item	My Prediction	How Many?

Data Collection Mini-Books: Science, Math, and Social Studies © 2007 by Joan Novelli, Scholastic Teaching Resources   page 18

Data Collection Mini-Books: Science, Math, and Social Studies © 2007 by Joan Novelli, Scholastic Teaching Resources

What's in the Lost and Found?

Fill in the chart to predict how many
backpacks  .

Color a backpack for each one you find.

Fill in the chart to tell how many backpacks.

Item	My Prediction	How Many?
Backpacks		

1. Look at the chart on page 11. Number the items from most to fewest.

_____ hats

_____ shoes

_____ jackets

_____ lunch boxes

_____ books

_____ backpacks

_____

2. There were more _____

than _____ .

3. Something else I learned about the

Lost and Found: _____

_____

Data Collection Mini-Books: Science, Math, and Social Studies © 2007 by Joan Novelli, Scholastic Teaching Resources   page 19

Data Collection Mini-Books: Science, Math, and Social Studies © 2007 by Joan Novelli, Scholastic Teaching Resources

What's in the Lost and Found?

Item		Total
Hats		
Shoes		
Jackets		
Lunch Boxes		
Books		
Backpacks		

What's in a Name?

Children sort and graph letters in their name, and compare them with other names in the class.

Teaching With the Mini-Book

1. On page 2 of the mini-book, have students write their name and color each letter in their name. For example, Renee would color in one *r*, one *n*, and one *e*. They should count each letter only once, no matter how many times it appears in the name. At the bottom of page 2, ask students to write the total number of letters in their name. (*Renee* would be five letters here.)

2. On page 3, have students color and total all the letters that are not in their name. On pages 4 and 5, have children color in first the vowels in their name and then the consonants. The same rule applies here as on page 2: Renee would color in only one *e*.

3. Referring to pages 4 and 5, invite students to complete the chart on page 6 by coloring in all cells up to and including the number they are representing.

4. Ask each student to work with a classmate to fill in the chart on page 7, coloring the cells up to and including the number they are representing on the chart. Invite children to continue the work with their classmates as they record what they learned on page 8 of the mini-book.

Extending Students' Learning

*   **Count All the Letters:** Let children compile their data to see how many different vowels and consonants are in everyone's names all together. Make a large alphabet chart. Invite children, one at a time, to call out the letters in their name as you circle them on the chart. Together, count how many letters are circled/not circled. Students can compare their individual data (from page 2) with the class data.

*   **Data Displays:** Discuss ways to display the mini-book data—for example, with a Venn diagram. Students can also manipulate letter tiles to sort letters in their names by vowels and consonants. Or they can use tally marks on a chart labeled "Vowels" and "Consonants" to count up how many of each.

Getting Started

Ahead of time, generate a conversation with students about consonants and vowels. List vowels and consonants for children to refer to, if needed, during the mini-book activity. Encourage children to make a quick estimate of how many vowels and consonants their name has. As an introduction, consider reading *Chrysanthemum*, by Kevin Henkes (see below).

Book Links

Chrysanthemum by Kevin Henkes (Greenwillow Books, 1991). Chrysanthemum loved her name until she started school and children teased her.

My Name Is Yoon by Helen Recorvits (Farrar, Straus and Giroux, 2003). A young Korean girl known as Yoon or "Shining Wisdom" tries to adjust to her new life and name in America.

What's in a Name?

Name _____

Date _____

(1)

Data Collection Mini-Books: Science, Math, and Social Studies © 2007 by Constance J. Leuenberger, Scholastic Teaching Resources

My name is _____ .

Color the letters that are in your name.

A B C D E F G H I
J K L M N O P Q R
S T U V W X Y Z

There are a total of _____ letters in my name.

(2)

Color the letters that are not in your name.

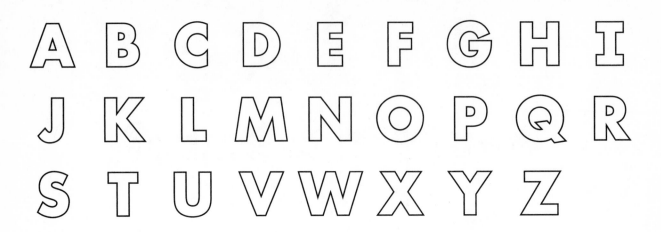

_____ letters are not in my name.

3

Data Collection Mini-Books: Science, Math, and Social Studies © 2007 by Constance J. Leuenberger, Scholastic Teaching Resources   page 22

Data Collection Mini-Books: Science, Math, and Social Studies © 2007 by Constance J. Leuenberger, Scholastic Teaching Resources

Color the vowels that are in your name.

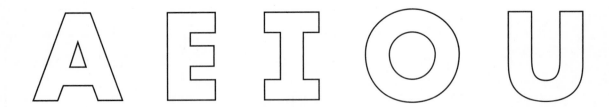

There are _____ vowels in my name.

_____ vowels are not in my name.

4

Color the consonants that are in your name.

B C D F G H J K L
M N P Q R S T V W
X Y Z

There are _____ consonants in my name.

_____ consonants are not in my name.

5

Data Collection Mini-Books: Science, Math, and Social Studies © 2007 by Constance J. Leuenberger, Scholastic Teaching Resources

Color in a space for each different vowel and consonant in your name.

Number of Different Vowels	**Number of Different Consonants**

Letters in My Name

6

Fill in the chart to compare data with two classmates.

Vowels	**Consonants**	**Vowels**	**Consonants**	**Vowels**	**Consonants**
Name:		Name:		Name:	

Number of Different Letters in My Name

7

Data Collection Mini-Books: Science, Math, and Social Studies © 2007 by Constance J. Leuenberger, Scholastic Teaching Resources

Look at the chart on page 7.

1. How many letters does the longest name have? _____

2. How many letters does the shortest name have? _____

3. Whose name has the most consonants? _____

4. What else does your chart tell you? _____

_____

_____.

8

Measure the School

Using footsteps as nonstandard measurement, children measure distances between points in school.

Teaching With the Mini-Book

1. Look at the chart on page 2 of the mini-book; invite students to estimate how many giant steps it will take for them to get from the classroom to each place listed. Have them fill in the chart under "My Estimate." If needed, remind children of the size of the footsteps they used in Getting Started.

2. Invite children to take and count giant steps to the places listed on the chart on page 2 (use the blank row to add a new location to the chart if desired), and record their answers in the appropriate column. Have them complete page 3 of the mini-book in the same manner as page 2 for measurements with tiny steps.

3. Invite students to try a new kind of step to complete page 4 of the mini-book. Have them record the type of step, estimate, and actual number of steps.

4. Use the chart on page 5 to compare data. Consider the differences in the number of steps it took to get from the classroom to each place. How does the data change with the type of step (giant, tiny)? Are the differences surprising? What accounts for the differences? Is this an exact measurement? Invite children to compare their page 5 charts with one another's. Use their responses on page 6 to guide a discussion about why children's numbers might be different.

Extending Students' Learning

- **Try It Again:** Invite students to walk to the same places, using the same steps, and record the numbers next to the ones in the mini-book. Did they get the same number of steps the second time? Why or why not? Invite students to come up with and test ideas for more exact measurement (for example, using a yardstick).

- **Taking It Further:** Revisit the charts in the mini-book. Encourage children to use their data to estimate how many steps it would take to get to different places—for example, "If it took 25 giant steps to get to the library, how many giant steps would it take to get to the _____ ?"

Getting Started

Explain that children will be measuring the school using different-sized footsteps. Note that taking uniform-sized footsteps for each activity will make the measurement more accurate. Practice taking tiny steps together, and then giant steps, and so on. Practice measuring short distances in the classroom, while emphasizing taking steps that are about the same size.

Book Links

How Big Is a Foot? by Rolf Myller (Dell, 1962). When the king orders a bed built, confusion erupts about whose foot to use for the measurements: the king's or the carpenter's.

How Tall? How Short? How Far Away? by David A. Adler (Holiday House, 1999). Explore measurement systems, including how they were developed and how measurements became standardized.

Estimate how many giant steps from your classroom to each place. Take giant steps. Fill in the chart.

Number of Giant Steps

Place	My Estimate	Number of Steps
Nearest Bathroom		
Nearest Exit		
Principal's Office		
Library		
Cafeteria		

2

Measure the School

Name _____

Date _____

1

Think of another kind of step you can take.

I will take _____ steps.

Fill in the chart to tell how many steps.

Number of _____ Steps

Place	My Estimate	Number of Steps
Nearest Bathroom		
Nearest Exit		
Principal's Office		
Library		
Cafeteria		

Data Collection Mini-Books: Science, Math, and Social Studies © 2007 by Constance J. Leuenberger, Scholastic Teaching Resources

Estimate how many tiny steps from your classroom to each place. Take tiny steps.

Fill in the chart.

Number of Tiny Steps

Place	My Estimate	Number of Steps
Nearest Bathroom		
Nearest Exit		
Principal's Office		
Library		
Cafeteria		

Compare one row of your chart with a classmate's chart.

1. We compared steps to _____ .
   place

2. My classmate had _____ giant steps.

3. I had _____ giant steps.

4. My classmate had _____ tiny steps.

5. I had _____ tiny steps.

6. Did you have the same number of steps as your classmate?

   Why or why not? _____

   _____

Data Collection Mini-Books: Science, Math, and Social Studies © 2007 by Constance J. Leuenberger, Scholastic Teaching Resources   page 28

Data Collection Mini-Books: Science, Math, and Social Studies © 2007 by Constance J. Leuenberger, Scholastic Teaching Resources

Look at pages 2, 3, and 4. Fill in the chart.

Comparing Information

Place	Number of Giant Steps	Number of Tiny Steps	Number of ____ Steps
Nearest Bathroom			
Nearest Exit			
Principal's Office			
Library			
Cafeteria			

Seasons Full of Birthdays

Children explore birthdays and the seasons in which they fall as they collect, organize, and represent data about these special days.

Teaching With the Mini-Book

1. After making sure students understand which season their birthday is in (see Getting Started), invite them to circle the season in which their birthday falls and make predictions about the birthdays in their class (page 2).

2. Next, have students interview classmates about their birthday seasons and use tallies to record this information on page 3 (see mini-lesson, page 7). Provide a class list so that students can check off classmates' names as they interview them.

3. Invite children to count and total the numbers on the sorting chart and write the totals on page 4 of the mini-book.

4. Encourage students to represent the information on page 4 in a different way by making a birthday graph on page 5. Children should color in each cell up to and including the number representing the total number of birthdays in each season.

5. On the last page of the mini-book, invite students to interpret the data they collected by answering the questions.

Extending Students' Learning

- **Sharing Information:** If possible, ask another class to complete the same mini-book. Then invite them to share their data with your class. Pair up children, one from each class. Ask children to compare and contrast the graphs on page 5 of their mini-books. Are they different or similar? What predictions can students make about birthday data from other classrooms?

- **What's Special About Seasons?** Invite children to take their explorations further by finding out what other special days fall in their birthday seasons. For example, is there a favorite holiday in their birthday season? How about a school vacation? What special people in history share their birthday month?

Getting Started

Make a four-column chart with the season names as headings (Fall, Winter, Spring, Summer). Under each season, list the dates that comprise it (for example, September 22–December 21 for fall). This provides a guide students can use when determining their birthday season. Display a chart of the months as an additional reference.

Book Links

The Reasons for Seasons by Gail Gibbons (Holiday House, 1995). This informative book succinctly explains seasons, including the earth's tilt and orbit, and what people and animals do each season.

The Shortest Day: Celebrating the Winter Solstice by Wendy Pfeffer (Dutton, 2003). This book offers a scientific explanation for the winter solstice, and introduces various cultures' beliefs about the seasons.

Circle the season in which your birthday falls.

Winter   **Spring**   **Summer**   **Fall**

1. In which season do you think you will find the most birthdays in your class?

_____

_____

2. In which season do you think you will find the fewest birthdays in your class?

_____

_____

2

Seasons Full of Birthdays

Name _____

Date _____

1

Count the number of birthdays in each season.
Fill in the chart to tell how many.

Season	Total
❄ Winter	
🌸 Spring	
☀ Summer	
🍂 Fall	

4

Tally how many classmates' birthdays are in each season. Use the sorting chart.

❄ Winter	🌸 Spring
☀ Summer	🍂 Fall

3

1. Look at the graph on page 5. In which season are the most birthdays?

_____

In which season are the fewest birthdays?

_____
_____

2. Compare your predictions on page 2 with your data on page 5. What did you learn about your predictions?

_____
_____
_____

3. What is surprising about the birthdays in your classroom?

_____
_____
_____

Make a graph of the birthdays in your class.

Birthday Graph

Number of Birthdays	Winter	Spring	Summer	Fall
9				
8				
7				
6				
5				
4				
3				
2				
1				
0				

Season

How Are Trees Alike?
How Are Trees Different?

In this mini-book, children compare and contrast the properties of three different trees.

Teaching With the Mini-Book

1. Take the class outside to the tree area, and invite children to observe their tree, taking note of its size, bark, leaves, and color.

2. On page 2 of the mini-book, have students make a bark rubbing of their tree (using crayons). Have children complete pages 2 through 4 by studying and recording information about the bark, leaves, and size of their tree.

3. Invite students to compare the bark, leaves, and sizes of the three trees on pages 5 and 6 of the mini-book.

4. On page 7, have students compare the sizes of the three trees, then compare the trees to other objects of their choosing.

5. Have students draw a picture of all three trees (page 8), using details to include as much scientific information as possible, and then compare the trees.

Note: Review the following information about leaf types to support students in completing the mini-book.

Smooth   Wavy

Lobed   Toothed

Extending Students' Learning

- **My Tree Through the Seasons:** Solidify the concepts in the mini-book by making the study of trees a year-round event. With each new season, invite students to complete a tree mini-book. At the end of the year, compare and contrast changes. How have the trees changed? Have they grown? What are the most striking differences in the tree over the seasons?

- **Plant a Tree:** Visit the National Arbor Day Foundation at arborday.org and learn how your class can help the environment by planting more trees. When you join the foundation, they will send you ten free trees that you and your students can plant!

Getting Started

Choose a safe outdoor place that has at least three trees. Divide the class into three groups, inviting each group to study a different tree. Provide pencils and crayons, flexible measuring tapes to measure the circumference of trees (or string to take the first measurement, and a measuring tape to convert that to standard measurements), and clipboards (or another surface on which students can write while observing the trees).

Book Links

Leaf Man by Lois Ehlert (Harcourt, 2005). In this adventure, a leaf man goes "where the wind blows." Animals and objects along the way are fashioned from leaves, identified in a leaf guide at the end of the book.

Tell Me Tree: All About Trees for Kids by Gail Gibbons (Little, Brown and Company, 2002). This oversized book discusses parts of trees and their functions, and tells how to identify trees by their leaves and bark.

How Are Trees Alike?
How Are Trees Different?

Name _____

Date _____

1

The Bark on My Tree

1. The bark feels _____

_____.

2. The bark is the color _____.

3. Something else I notice about the bark

is that it _____

My Bark Rubbing

_____.

2

The Leaves on My Tree

Draw your leaf.

1. Words that describe the shape

of the leaf: _____

_____ .

2. Words that describe the colors

in the leaf: _____

_____ .

3

 **The Size of My Tree**

1. The circumference of my tree is _____
inches near the ground.

2. My tree is taller than _____ .

3. My tree is shorter than _____ .

4

Comparing the Bark of Trees

Question	Tree 1	Tree 2	Tree 3
What does the bark feel like?	_____ Smooth _____ Rough _____ Other (explain) _____	_____ Smooth _____ Rough _____ Other (explain) _____	_____ Smooth _____ Rough _____ Other (explain) _____
What color is the bark?	_____ More green _____ More brown _____ More gray _____ Other (explain) _____	_____ More green _____ More brown _____ More gray _____ Other (explain) _____	_____ More green _____ More brown _____ More gray _____ Other (explain) _____

5

Data Collection Mini-Books: Science, Math, and Social Studies © 2007 by Constance J. Leuenberger, Scholastic Teaching Resources   page 36

Data Collection Mini-Books: Science, Math, and Social Studies © 2007 by Constance J. Leuenberger, Scholastic Teaching Resources

Comparing the Leaves of Trees

Question	Tree 1	Tree 2	Tree 3
What color are the leaves?	_____ Red _____ Orange _____ Yellow _____ Brown _____ Green	_____ Red _____ Orange _____ Yellow _____ Brown _____ Green	_____ Red _____ Orange _____ Yellow _____ Brown _____ Green
What shape are the leaves?	_____ Smooth _____ Lobed _____ Wavy _____ Toothed	_____ Smooth _____ Lobed _____ Wavy _____ Toothed	_____ Smooth _____ Lobed _____ Wavy _____ Toothed

6

Comparing the Size of Trees

1. The largest circumference of the trees we studied is _____ inches.

2. The smallest circumference of the trees we studied is _____ inches.

3. The difference between the two circumferences is _____ .

4. The tallest tree is taller than _____ .

5. The shortest tree is taller than _____ .

7

Draw a picture of each tree.

Tree 1	Tree 2	Tree 3

1. How are the trees alike? _____

2. How are the trees different? _____

8

Eating Lunch With the Five Food Groups

Children become nutritionists as they collect data about the five food groups and lunches served in the school cafeteria.

Teaching With the Mini-Book

1. Introduce children to the five food groups. Make a list of the food groups and examples of different foods for each category. Have students look at page 2, and draw a new food in each group. Use this page as a guide for the research students will be conducting over the course of five days in the school cafeteria.

2. Have children complete a chart for each of five days, coloring one picture for each food served. Keep in mind that the pictures in the charts are merely symbols that represent each food group. For example, if rice and noodles are served on day one, students color two bread pictures to represent two foods from the breads and grains food group. If apples and bananas are on the menu one day, they color two bananas in the fruit group to indicate that two fruits were served.

3. After completing five days of research, have students examine the data collected, counting how many foods in each food group were served over the course of the five days. Students record these numbers on the chart on page 8.

4. On page 9, children compare the food groups that were served in the cafeteria, recording what the cafeteria served the most and least of. Students record what they learned at the bottom of page 9. On page 10, children culminate what they have learned by drawing a picture of their favorite meal, showing something from each of the five food groups.

Extending Students' Learning

Take It Home: Provide students with a second copy of the mini-book, and invite them to try this activity at home. Compare and contrast the two mini-books and discuss how students can make healthy food choices at home and at school.

Getting Started

Be sure to let the cafeteria staff know that your class will be conducting a survey about the five food groups served at lunchtime. If possible, arrange for a time (other than children's actual lunchtime) each day during a week when students can collect data about the day's lunch. If there is not a time for students to collect data in the cafeteria, collect the data from the school lunch menu.

Book Links

Eat Healthy, Feel Great by William and Martha Sears (Little, Brown Young Readers, 2002). This book gives children tools to make wise food choices and includes kid-friendly recipes.

Good Enough to Eat: A Kid's Guide to Food and Nutrition by Lizzy Rockwell (HarperCollins, 1999). This informative picture book introduces nutrition and explains the process of digestion.

Eating Lunch With the Five Food Groups

Name _____

Date _____

1

Data Collection Mini-Books: Science, Math, and Social Studies © 2007 by Constance J. Leuenberger, Scholastic Teaching Resources

Draw a new food in each group.

Breads and Grains	Fruits	Vegetables	Protein	Dairy

Which food group do you think the cafeteria serves the most of?

_____

2

Day 1

For each food in the cafeteria today, color a picture in the matching food group.

Breads and Grains	Fruits	Vegetables	Protein	Dairy

3

Day 2

For each food in the cafeteria today, color a picture in the matching food group.

Breads and Grains	Fruits	Vegetables	Protein	Dairy

4

Day 3

For each food in the cafeteria today, color a picture in the matching food group.

Breads and Grains	Fruits	Vegetables	Protein	Dairy

5

Day 4

For each food in the cafeteria today, color a picture in the matching food group.

Breads and Grains	Fruits	Vegetables	Protein	Dairy

6

Day 5

For each food in the cafeteria today, color a picture in the matching food group.

Breads and Grains	Fruits	Vegetables	Protein	Dairy

7

Use pages 2–7 to complete the chart.

Food Group	Total
Breads and Grains	
Fruits	
Vegetables	
Protein	
Dairy	

8

1. Which food group did the cafeteria serve the most of?

_____

2. Which food group did the cafeteria serve the least of?

_____

3. What did you learn about the food the cafeteria serves?

_____

_____

9

Data Collection Mini-Books: Science, Math, and Social Studies © 2007 by Constance J. Leuenberger, Scholastic Teaching Resources

Draw a picture of your favorite meal. Label the food groups.

10

Discovering Rocks

Students use the skills of weighing, measuring, and comparing in this mini-book about rocks.

Teaching With the Mini-Book

1. Give each student a sheet of paper. Have children divide the paper into three sections and label them 1, 2, 3. Have children place one rock on each section. Encourage them to refer to each rock by this number while using the mini-book.

2. Have children draw a picture of their rocks on page 2. Remind them to draw like scientists, making their drawings look as much like the rocks as possible.

3. Using string, have children measure the circumference of their rocks by wrapping a string around the outside of each rock at the widest point and cutting (or marking) the string at the point where the two ends meet. Have children use a ruler to measure the string and then record this standard measurement (page 3). At the bottom of the page, invite students to compare the size of the rocks.

4. On page 4 children organize their data to display circumferences from largest to smallest (a good time to reinforce math language for comparisons).

5. Using a scale, have children weigh their rocks, recording the weight on page 5. At the bottom of page 5, encourage children to make comparisons, listing three things that are heavier than their heaviest rock.

6. Ask children to notice the textures of their rocks and tally each texture found (page 6). They can use the blank space to add another texture. On page 7, invite students to draw and write about their favorite rock, using plenty of details.

7. Finally, on page 8, ask students to transfer their study of rocks beyond the rocks they've collected. Have them consider things around the school that are made from rock (such as drainage ditches around the school or a rock walkway), as well as other uses for rocks, and then record their ideas.

Extending Students' Learning

- **Rock Swap:** Invite another class to collect rocks. Pair students, one from each class, and have them trade rocks and then test them in the same manner as in the mini-book.

- **Sorting and Classifying:** Use string to make a Venn diagram on the floor. Let children sort the rocks (for example, by circumference, color, texture, or weight).

Getting Started

As a homework activity, ask students to collect three different types of small rocks and bring them to school. Before starting the mini-book, invite children to bring their rocks to a circle on the floor. Ask students to put their rocks in front of them so everyone can see all the rocks. Together, generate a list of everything students notice about the rocks, and things they know about rocks in general.

Book Links

Rocks and Minerals by Steve Parker (DK Publishing, 1993). Colorful pictures and lots of factual information make this book a favorite for children to browse.

Rocks and Minerals by Tracy Staedter (Reader's Digest, 1999). Vivid pictures with detailed descriptions explain the facts about rocks and minerals.

Collect three rocks.

Draw a picture of each rock.

Rock	Picture of My Rock
Rock 1	
Rock 2	
Rock 3	

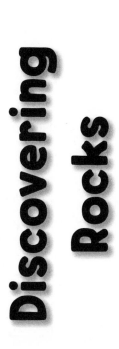

Discovering Rocks

Name _____

Date _____

Look at page 3. Put your rocks in order from largest to smallest.

Rock	Circumference
Largest Rock	
Next Largest Rock	
Smallest Rock	

4

Data Collection Mini-Books: Science, Math, and Social Studies © 2007 by Constance J. Leuenberger, Scholastic Teaching Resources

Circumference

Measure the circumference of each rock.

Rock	Circumference
Rock 1	
Rock 2	
Rock 3	

1. Rock number _____ is bigger than rock number _____.

2. Rock number _____ is _____ than rock number _____.

3

Texture

Tally the textures found in your rocks.

Texture	Tally	Total
Smooth		
Rough		
Bumpy		
Has Holes		

6

Weight

Weigh your rocks.

Rock	Weight
Rock 1	
Rock 2	
Rock 3	

Name three things that are heavier than your heaviest rock.

_____

_____

_____

5

Rocks Everywhere

1. Where are rocks used around your

school? _____

_____

_____

_____

2. What are some other uses for rocks?

_____

_____

_____

_____

My Favorite Rock

Draw a picture of your favorite rock.

1. My favorite rock is about as big as

_____ .

2. Words that describe my favorite rock are

_____

_____ .

How Many Water Drops?

Children explore the surface tension of water as they predict and test how many water drops will fit on a coin.

Teaching With the Mini-Book

1. Generate discussion about how many water drops might fit on a penny. Two? Thirty? One hundred? Have children make and record predictions, test them, and record results (page 2).

2. Continue with pages 3 through 5 in the same manner. Children can use the data they gather in each test to predict how many drops will fit on each type of coin.

3. Have children organize their data on pages 6 and 7 of the mini-book, and then complete page 8 to make predictions based on their data.

Extending Students' Learning

- **The Science Behind the Experiments:** Inside a water drop, the water molecules are strongly attracted to each other. This attraction is called cohesion. As children drop water on a coin, drop by drop, cohesion tugs at the molecules on the surface, pulling them in from the sides and downward. This creates surface tension, which acts like a skin to hold the drop together as it gets bigger and bigger. (You might invite children to recall observations of bugs sitting on top of water and explain that it is the skinlike property of water that allows them to do this.) As more drops of water are added, the force of gravity becomes stronger than the force of attraction among the water molecules, causing the water to roll off the coin or surface. Larger coins have more surface area than smaller coins. Coins with lots of detail provide more surface area than coins with little detail. Hence, the larger the coin, and the more detailed, the more water drops it will hold.

- **Reduce Surface Tension:** Invite students to try the experiments in the mini-book again, but this time with soapy water. (Adding soap reduces the surface tension; therefore, students may find that coins hold fewer drops of soapy water.)

- **Making More Inferences:** After students have had a chance to see how water drops react on a coin, invite them to test their inferences in different ways. Have students experiment with water drops on waxed paper, aluminum foil, sandpaper, and paper towels. Do the water drops act differently on different surfaces? On which surface do the water drops hold together best?

Book Link

A Drop of Water: A Book of Science and Wonder by Walter Wick (Scholastic, 1997). Wick encourages readers to discover the magical properties of water through fun, educational experiments.

How many water drops fit on a penny?

My prediction: _____

My count: _____

What is the difference between your prediction and your count? Complete the number sentence to show your answer.

_____ − _____ = _____

Was your prediction more than, less than, or equal to your count?

☐ more than   ☐ less than

☐ equal to

Data Collection Mini-Books: Science, Math, and Social Studies © 2007 by Constance J. Leuenberger, Scholastic Teaching Resources   page 50

Data Collection Mini-Books: Science, Math, and Social Studies © 2007 by Constance J. Leuenberger, Scholastic Teaching Resources

How Many Water Drops?

Name _____

Date _____

How many water drops fit on a dime?

My prediction: _____

My count: _____

What is the difference between your prediction and your count? Complete the number sentence to show your answer.

_____ - _____ = _____

Was your prediction more than, less than, or equal to your count?

☐ more than   ☐ less than

☐ equal to

4

Data Collection Mini-Books: Science, Math, and Social Studies © 2007 by Constance J. Leuenberger, Scholastic Teaching Resources

How many water drops fit on a nickel?

My prediction: _____

My count: _____

What is the difference between your prediction and your count? Complete the number sentence to show your answer.

_____ - _____ = _____

Was your prediction more than, less than, or equal to your count?

☐ more than   ☐ less than

☐ equal to

3

Fill in the chart. Draw a circle around the coin that held the most water drops. Draw a square around the coin that held the fewest water drops.

Coin	Number of Drops
Penny	
Nickel	
Dime	
Quarter	

How many water drops fit on a quarter?

My prediction: _____

My count: _____

What is the difference between your prediction and your count? Complete the number sentence to show your answer.

_____ – _____ = _____

Was your prediction more than, less than, or equal to your count?

☐ more than

☐ less than

☐ equal to

1. Do you think five different pennies would all hold the same number of water drops?

_____

Test your idea. Write about your results.

_____

_____

2. Why do you think some coins might hold more water drops than others?

_____

_____

_____

Data Collection Mini-Books: Science, Math, and Social Studies © 2007 by Constance J. Leuenberger, Scholastic Teaching Resources   page 53

Data Collection Mini-Books: Science, Math, and Social Studies © 2007 by Constance J. Leuenberger, Scholastic Teaching Resources

1. Look at the chart on page 6. Number the coins from 1 to 4 to show most to fewest drops of water.

 _____ penny

 _____ nickel

 _____ dime

 _____ quarter

2. The _____ held more water drops than the _____.

Will It Sink? Will It Float?

The property of buoyancy is explored in this mini-book as children use objects in a sink or float experiment.

Teaching With the Mini-Book

1. Before beginning the experiment, ask children to predict which items will sink or float and to use words or pictures to record their predictions on page 2.

2. Invite students to test the items for buoyancy in a tub of water, recording the results on pages 3 and 4.

3. When all items have been tested for buoyancy and recorded in the mini-book, have children complete page 5, creating a hypothesis to explain why things sink or float.

4. On the last page of the mini-book, have students compare their predictions to results and then generate other ideas of things that will sink or float. Be sure to note the possibility that a child's predictions may have all been correct, which will eliminate the need to complete the first two parts of this page.

Extending Students' Learning

- **Saltwater or Freshwater?** Have children consider what they discovered about buoyancy and then predict whether an egg will sink or float in water (repeat with saltwater). Place an egg in water to test students' predictions. Gradually add teaspoons of salt to the glass of water to see if the results change. (At first an egg will sink; then as salt is added, it will eventually float because the density of water is increased as salt is added.) Keeping the experiment in mind, ask students if they think it is easier to float in an ocean or a lake.

- **Retesting Our Findings:** Ask children to revisit the items they tested for buoyancy. While keeping in mind the experiment with the egg (above), ask children to predict whether or not objects that previously sank would float in saltwater. Let children test their ideas. Did saltwater make a difference? If so, how much salt was needed before the objects floated? Encourage children to record their findings by completing a second mini-book for saltwater or by adding to the original mini-book.

Getting Started

Ahead of time, set up an activity center with a tub of water and several items that will sink or float. Suggested items include a sponge, wooden block, shell, rock, pinecone, waxed paper, cork, key, nail, empty plastic bottle, stick, bottle cap, crayon, and paper clip. Include two large sheets of paper, one titled "Sinks" and one titled "Floats," for children to place items on accordingly.

Book Links

Let's Try It Out in the Water by Seymour Simon and Nicole Fauteaux (Simon and Schuster, 2001). This activity-based book helps the young scientist understand buoyancy, air pressure, and gravity.

Splish! Splosh! Why Do We Wash? by Janice Lobb (Kingfisher, 2000). Twelve easy experiments explore questions such as why boats float, why water turns cold, and why mirrors steam up.

1. What do you think will sink?

2. What do you think will float?

Data Collection Mini-Books: Science, Math, and Social Studies © 2007 by Constance J. Leuenberger, Scholastic Teaching Resources

Will It Sink?
Will It Float?

Name _____

Date _____

Record each item you tested.
Check the box to tell if it sinks or floats.

Item Name	Sinks	Floats

Data Collection Mini-Books: Science, Math, and Social Studies © 2007 by Constance J. Leuenberger, Scholastic Teaching Resources   page 56

Data Collection Mini-Books: Science, Math, and Social Studies © 2007 by Constance J. Leuenberger, Scholastic Teaching Resources

1. What sinks?
Draw a picture of the things that sink.
Label your pictures.

2. What floats?
Draw a picture of the things that float.
Label your pictures.

6

1. I thought a _____ would sink. But it floats.

2. I thought a _____ would float. But it sinks.

3. These are other things I think will sink:

_____

_____

4. These are other things I think will float:

_____

_____

5. Test your ideas.

5

1. I think things sink because _____

_____

_____

2. I think things float because _____

_____

_____

School Helpers

A survey helps students understand the many different jobs helpers in the school perform.

Teaching With the Mini-Book

1. Encourage students to use the class list of helpers to complete page 2.

2. Have children conduct interviews with school helpers, completing the charts on pages 3 and 4. Customize the headings on page 3 as necessary to best fit the job descriptions at your school. Guide children in completing the headings on page 4 with additional job descriptions. For each chart, children can check as many boxes as apply to each helper.

3. Support students as needed to answer questions and formulate ideas based on the data they've collected as they complete the mini-book.

Extending Students' Learning

- **Sharing Results:** Using the charts on pages 3 and 4, invite students to share what they learned. Allow time for questioning from other students: Discussion about data analysis and representation helps clear up misconceptions and allows for new learning and instruction.

- **Helping Out:** After children have reviewed and discussed the data they gathered in the mini-book, ask them if there is a job they learned about that they would like to know more about. If possible, arrange to have students be "helpers" to a school worker for a short period of time. This will help your students understand the work that is put forth every day in order to make everyone's day successful. This will also help forge some new relationships for your students that they may cherish forever. After students have tried out some of the jobs, they may want to institute a "staff appreciation" day. For this event, students can deliver handmade gifts and cards to the many staff members in the school, showing their appreciation. A staff appreciation tea or breakfast is always a welcome idea as well.

Getting Started

Before children interview helpers in the school, generate a class list of the different helpers in your school and the jobs they do. When interviewing school helpers, you may want to have children work in pairs. Invite school workers into the classroom for interviews. If children will be interviewing workers throughout the school, it's a good idea to ask the workers ahead of time.

Book Links

Hooray for Diffendoofer Day by Jack Prelutsky (Knopf, 1998). Based on drawings and verses from Dr. Seuss, this book is an ode to creative teachers, school staff, and children everywhere!

I Want to Be a Teacher by Daniel Liebman (Firefly Books, 2001). Full-page, color photographs depict teachers of many cultures as they perform their jobs and duties of the day.

School Helpers

Name _____

Date _____

1

Who are some helpers you know in your school?

_____

_____

What are some jobs helpers do in your school?

_____

_____

2

Take a survey of school helpers. Check the boxes to tell how they help.

Name of Helper	Cleans the School	Teaches	Helps in the Cafeteria	Helps on the Playground

3

Make a new chart. Fill in more jobs helpers do.

Name of Helper				

4

1. How many helpers do more than one job? _____

_____

2. What other jobs does a teacher have? _____

_____

3. Name a worker who helps in more than one place in the school.

_____

5

What is a way you help at your school?

Draw a picture.   Write about it.

_____

_____

_____

_____

6

Fire Safety

Students set out on a scavenger hunt to find fire safety tools in the school.

Teaching With the Mini-Book

1. Generate a discussion about fire safety in school, reviewing fire drill plans and escape routes. If possible, invite the local fire department in to explain to children the importance of fire safety. It's a good idea to invite firefighters to suit up and demonstrate what they will look like in the event of a real fire. Awareness of what to expect will help children understand the situation better and be calmer about it. Of course, a field trip to the fire station is always a good precursor to a study of fire safety.

2. Invite students to check for fire safety tools in the following areas of school: the classroom, cafeteria, gym, and hallway. As they gather data in each area, children can check off the items they see (pages 2 through 5).

3. Encourage children to revisit pages 2 through 5, counting the check marks for each area of the school. On page 6 of the mini-book, have students record the total number of checks for each area of the school. At the bottom of the page, students can analyze the data, using the number of checks to tell which area of the school has the most/fewest types of fire safety tools. Encourage students to summarize what they learned from their research.

4. Generate a discussion about other places students might see fire safety tools, such as at home, on the bus, at the doctor's office, or in a store.

Extending Students' Learning

- **Map It:** Using a fire escape map from your classroom as a model, invite students to make their own fire safety maps, adding details of their own.

- **Use It at Home:** Encourage students and families to talk about fire safety at home, coming up with a plan in case of fire. The local fire department may have recommendations to share with families about this—for example, that each family have an escape plan and a place to meet. Be sure that students know standard fire safety rules.

Getting Started

Point out the fire safety tools included in the mini-book. Explain the function of each fire safety tool, highlighting that these tools keep people safe. It is important that students understand that these tools are to be used only during a fire, and can be dangerous if used when not needed. Before children complete the mini-book, let school staff know to expect to find students in the hall gathering data.

Book Links

Officer Buckle and Gloria by Peggy Rathman (Putnam, 1995). In this Caldecott Medal book, Officer Buckle's safety speeches to the local schoolchildren are very dull, until his police dog, Gloria, is invited along.

Stop Drop and Roll by Margery Cuyler (Simon and Schuster, 2001). Jessica learns how to keep her home fire-safe during fire prevention week at school.

Look at the fire safety tools below.
Check the ones you see in your classroom:

☐ Fire Extinguisher

☐ Fire Alarm

☐ Exit Sign

FIRE EXIT

☐ Escape Map

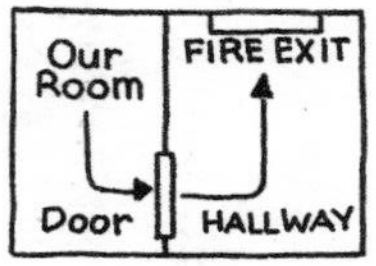

Our Room → Door → FIRE EXIT → HALLWAY

☐ Other _____

2

Fire Safety

Name _____

Date _____

1

Look at the fire safety tools below.
Check the ones you see in the gym:

☐ Fire Extinguisher

☐ Fire Alarm

☐ Exit Sign

☐ Escape Map

☐ Other _____

4

Look at the fire safety tools below.
Check the ones you see in the cafeteria:

☐ Fire Extinguisher

☐ Fire Alarm

☐ Exit Sign

☐ Escape Map

☐ Other _____

3

How many checks in each area?

_____ Classroom

_____ Cafeteria

_____ Gym

_____ Hallway

In which area(s) did you find the most types
of fire safety tools?

_____

In which area(s) did you find the fewest
types of fire safety tools?

_____

6

Data Collection Mini-Books: Science, Math, and Social Studies © 2007 by Constance J. Leuenberger, Scholastic Teaching Resources

Look at the fire safety tools below.
Check the ones you see in the hallway:

☐ Fire Extinguisher

☐ Fire Alarm

☐ Exit Sign

☐ Escape Map

☐ Other _____

5

Mapping the School

Mapping skills combine with data collection in a mini-book that invites students to map different areas of the school.

Getting Started

Make simplified maps of the playground, cafeteria, classroom, and main office. Be sure these will fit on pages 2 through 5 of the mini-book. Glue these into the corresponding mini-book pages to make a master; then photocopy a class set. The book *Me on the Map*, by Joan Sweeney (Crown, 1996), offers great examples of simple maps of the narrator's room, house, and town. Share this book with students before starting the mini-book.

Teaching With the Mini-Book

1. Before working on the mini-book, look at different types of maps with students. Commercial maps are worth looking at, because students will use these maps as they get older. Also make some simplified maps depicting places children are familiar with, such as an area of your town with a park. Consider taking a look at the emergency exit maps for your school. Students may be familiar with these from the fire safety mini-book. (See page 62.)

2. Invite children to take a look around the school, comparing the maps in their mini-books with the actual places. In the process, point out the orientation of the maps and help students become familiar with the features of each.

3. Encourage students to further study the maps of places in the school on pages 2 through 5. Note that on each page, students are asked to use a symbol to designate a particular place on the map. Guide students in answering questions relating to each of the maps.

4. Foster children's own mapmaking skills using page 6 of the mini-book. Encourage them to draw their own map of a place at school that has not been mapped in the mini-book. Have them draw a circle around their favorite spot on the map they make and explain why they like that place. If children find this concept difficult, encourage them to practice drawing a map or two of familiar places on large paper until they feel more comfortable.

Extending Students' Learning

- **Recreating the Maps:** Using their mini-books as reference, have students experiment with creating representations of their maps with blocks or other building materials. Encourage students to consider orientation and features of their maps as they arrange the blocks.

- **Making It Real:** Invite students to share and use their map mini-books with their families. For example, students might share the maps with families at open school night to familiarize them with places in the school.

Book Links

Rosie's Walk by Pat Hutchins (Macmillan, 1968). Rosie the hen travels over, under, and around the barnyard, oblivious to a fox following her.

The Secret Birthday Message by Eric Carle (HarperTrophy, 1986). A boy follows directions in a secret message to find his birthday gift.

This is a map of the playground. Draw a ☐ around a favorite place to play.

Paste a map of the playground here.

1. The _____ is/are
   favorite place

   farthest away from the _____ .

2. The _____ is/are
   favorite place

   closest to the _____ .
   favorite place

Mapping the School

Name _____

Date _____

This is a map of the classroom.
Draw an **X** to show where you sit.

Paste a map of the classroom here.

Draw an O around your favorite part of the classroom. Why do you like this spot?

4

This is a map of the cafeteria.
Draw a ☆ to show where you sit.

Paste a map of the cafeteria here.

1. The _____ is/are closest to the _____ .

2. The _____ is/are farthest from the _____ .

3

Make a map of a place at your school that you have not mapped yet.

Paste your map here.

Draw an ◯ around your favorite place. What do you do in this place?

6

This is a map of the main office. Draw an ➝ to show where the principal works.

Paste a map of the main office here.

The _____

in the main office is behind the _____ .

5

Our Favorite Times

Surveying others about their favorite time of day, day of the week, month of the year, and season gives students some interesting information to analyze.

Teaching With the Mini-Book

1. Using the checklist on page 2 of the mini-book, invite students to check their favorite time of day. Encourage them to write about their favorite time of day at the bottom of the page.

2. Skipping pages, continue with pages 4, 6, and 8 of the mini-book. Invite children to check and write about their favorite day of the week, month, and season.

3. Next, encourage students to interview five people, asking them about their favorite time of day, day of the week, month, and season. Invite students to record their answers as tallies on pages 3, 5, 7, and 9 of the mini-book, respectively (see mini-lesson, page 7). Then have them compare their favorite day (week, month, season) with the data they collected.

4. Last, have students study the data they collected on pages 3, 5, 7, and 9 of the mini-book and answer the questions on page 10.

Extending Students' Learning

- **Survey Sharing:** Invite students to share their survey findings. Encourage discussion about the similarities and differences in the survey results. Pose questions, such as *Why do you think the survey results might be the same? Different? What does this have to do with the people you interviewed? Who would be interested in using this information?*

- **Show It Another Way:** Give each student a large sheet of white drawing paper. Have students fold the paper twice to make four squares, and then unfold it. Have them label the first square "Time of Day," the second square "Day of the Week," the third square "Month of the Year," and the fourth square "Season." Encourage students to draw a scene about each favorite time, telling why it is their favorite.

Getting Started

Ahead of time, consider whom students should survey for this mini-book. Will it serve the students better to interview classmates or adults? Would students gain more from doing this as a homework assignment or as an activity at school? In addition, generating conversation about days, months, and seasons will help students think about their own responses for the mini-book.

Book Links

Ma Dear's Aprons by Patrick McKissack (Atheneum, 1997). David Earl, a young African-American boy at the turn of the 20th century, recognizes the days of the week by his dear Ma's aprons.

Telling Time With Big Mama Cat by Dan Harper (Harcourt Brace, 1998). A cat leads a busy life of napping, eating, and napping some more. Readers can manipulate the hands of the movable clock on the book's cover.

Our Favorite Times

Name _____

Date _____

1

Data Collection Mini-Books: Science, Math, and Social Studies © 2007 by Constance J. Leuenberger, Scholastic Teaching Resources

Favorite Time of Day

Check your favorite time of day.

☐ Morning   ☐ Middle of the Day   ☐ Night

This is my favorite time of day because _____

_____.

2

Ask five people what their favorite time of day is. Tally.

Time	Tallies	Total
Morning		
Middle of the Day		
Night		

How does your favorite time of day compare with others'?

_____ .

3

Favorite Day

Check your favorite day of the week.

☐ Sunday   ☐ Tuesday   ☐ Friday

☐ Monday   ☐ Wednesday   ☐ Saturday

☐ Thursday

This is my favorite day because _____

_____ .

4

Ask five people what their favorite day of the week is. Tally.

How does your favorite day of the week compare with others'?

_____

_____ .

Day	Tallies	Total
Sunday		
Monday		
Tuesday		
Wednesday		
Thursday		
Friday		
Saturday		

5

Data Collection Mini-Books: Science, Math, and Social Studies © 2007 by Constance J. Leuenberger, Scholastic Teaching Resources

Favorite Month

☐ January   ☐ May   ☐ September

☐ February   ☐ June   ☐ October

☐ March   ☐ July   ☐ November

☐ April   ☐ August   ☐ December

This is my favorite month because _____

_____ .

6

Ask five people what their favorite month is. Tally.

Month	Tallies	Total	Month	Tallies	Total
January			July		
February			August		
March			September		
April			October		
May			November		
June			December		

How does your favorite month compare with others'?

_____ . 7

Data Collection Mini-Books: Science, Math, and Social Studies © 2007 by Constance J. Leuenberger, Scholastic Teaching Resources   page 74

Data Collection Mini-Books: Science, Math, and Social Studies © 2007 by Constance J. Leuenberger, Scholastic Teaching Resources

Favorite Season

Check your favorite season.

☐ Winter

☐ Summer

☐ Spring

☐ Fall

This is my favorite season because _____

_____ . 8

Ask five people what their favorite season is. Tally.

Season		Tallies	Total
Winter			
Spring			
Summer			
Fall			

How does your favorite season compare with others'?

_____ .

9

Survey Results

1. The most favorite time of day is _____ .

2. The most favorite day of the week is _____ .

3. The most favorite month is _____ .

4. The most favorite season is _____ .

5. Something else I learned from my surveys is that _____

_____ .

10

Our Favorite Authors

Students use a survey of classmates' favorite authors to practice the skills of data collection and organization.

Teaching With the Mini-Book

1. Begin with a class discussion about books by the authors listed in the mini-book. Ask questions, such as "What do you like about this book? Why?"

2. Invite students to draw a picture about their favorite book and record the author and title on page 2. This does not have to be a book by one of the featured authors. This is a springboard to get students talking about favorite books.

3. On page 3, have students put a check next to their favorite author and tell why they like this author.

4. Ask students to predict who they think will be the most popular author in your class. On page 4, invite them to give their reasons and name a book they have read (or would like to read) by that author. Then have students survey ten classmates about their favorite authors, tallying and totaling answers on page 5 (see mini-lesson, page 7).

5. Page 6 asks children to analyze the data and determine which author was most liked by the ten classmates. Students explain why they think this author was well liked, and write about their own favorite book by this author.

6. Encourage students to show the data a different way on page 7 by coloring in the squares to make a graph that depicts the number of votes each author received from the ten classmates. Finally, on page 8 students assess the survey by telling what surprised them.

Extending Students' Learning

A Larger Sample: What would happen if you gave 20 people the same survey? Thirty people? What if you asked people of a different grade or age? Would the results change? As a class, conduct the survey on different groups of people (such as students in an upper grade) and compare and contrast results.

Getting Started

It's a good idea to read aloud several books by the authors featured in this mini-book (see Book Links, below) so that students have a common understanding. Classroom displays featuring books by these authors will provide further support. Note that the mini-book includes a space for adding another author (page 3).

Book Links

Anansi Does the Impossible: An Ashanti Tale by Verna Aardema (Atheneum, 1997). Clever Anansi sets out to buy back all the folktales from the Sky God.

Arthur's Family Vacation by Marc Brown (Little, Brown, 1993). Arthur doesn't let a little rain spoil his family vacation.

Hedgie's Surprise by Jan Brett (Putnam, 2000). Hedgie the hedgehog helps Henny the Hen trick a mischievous Tomten out of stealing her eggs.

Strega Nona by Tomie dePaola (Simon and Schuster, 1975). In this Caldecott Honor book, Strega Nona gives Big Anthony a lesson in following directions.

Data Collection Mini-Books: Science, Math, and Social Studies Scholastic Teaching Resources

What's your favorite book?

Draw a picture about the book.

Write the title and author's name.

Title _____

Author _____

2

Our Favorite Authors

Name _____

Date _____

1

1. Which author do you think is most popular in your class?

_____

Why? _____

_____

2. Name a book you have read (or would like to read) by this author:

_____

_____

_____

These are some favorite children's authors:

• Marc Brown (Arthur books)

• Verna Aardema (Anansi books)

• Jan Brett (The Mitten)

• Tomie dePaola (Strega Nona)

• _____

Which of these authors is your favorite?

_____

Tell three things you like about this author.

1. _____

2. _____

3. _____

Look at the chart on page 5.

1. Which author has the most votes?

_____

2. Why do you think this author is so

well liked? _____

_____

3. What is your favorite book by this

author? _____

Why? _____

_____

6

Take a survey. Survey ten classmates about their favorite author. Fill in the chart.

Author	Tallies	Total
Marc Brown		
Verna Aardema		
Jan Brett		
Tomie dePaola		

5

1. What surprised you about this survey?

_____

_____

_____

2. Who do you think this survey might

help? _____

_____

Why? _____

_____

8

Look at page 5.
Use the data to make a graph.

	Marc Brown	Verna Aardema	Jan Brett	Tomie dePaola
10				
9				
8				
7				
6				
5				
4				
3				
2				
1				
0				

Number of Votes

Authors

7